LEMONADE...
and Other Stands We
Shouldn't Have Taken

2013

Compilation produced by Dandelion Wine Press
with express permissions by contributing authors

Lemonade…and Other Stands We Shouldn't Have Taken

Published by
Dandelion Wine Press
Copyright © 2013

DANDELION WINE PRESS, LTD
PO BOX 270787
LITTLETON, CO 80127
www.dandelionwine.co

Printed in the United States of America

2

TABLE OF CONTENTS

TABLE OF CONTENTS
CONTINUED

CAMPER CAPER

Back in the 90's, my husband and I found ourselves buying a twenty-four-foot behemoth that was cleverly disguised as a family camper. We had started out that day, "just looking." Suddenly, I was pulling cash out of my purse and handing it over to the stranger who stood grinning beside the camper.

What did we know about a twenty-four-foot behemoth, I worried in silence as the eager seller rattled off a glossary of terms I didn't understand.

"Black water, gray water, articulation point, payload, umbilical cord, blah, blah, blah." And what the hell is dry camping anyway?

What have we done? I asked myself as I stared down the monster in the peddler's driveway. Slowly, my husband crept down the driveway in our Blazer toward the beast. If I didn't know any better, I'd swear he was sneaking up on it. The next thing I remember was the massive appendage following us down the highway toward home. (If you have never seen the movie The Long, Long Trailer, I highly recommend it.)

A few days later, I began making new curtains and covers for the cushions. That 70's camper motif had to go; and the sooner, the better.

Me and my trailer soon bonded over several scrub pads and buckets of fresh cleaning solution. She was looking pretty nice and a sense of home was taking shape. Our two daughters, four and five years old, loved the trailer. It was a fun place for them to play while I sewed ten thousand more cushion covers.

Finally, our maiden voyage was upon us, from Colorado to the shores of Cape Hatteras, North Carolina. One would think a first voyage would be a short trek to the mountains or something; you know, to break her in and work out the kinks. Get to know her better at least. No, we chose cross country.

The glorious morning had arrived...we were to leave in just an hour for a three-week adventure, but we had a hitch in our get-along. No, literally, we had a hitch problem. So my husband had to haul the camper up the road for a hitch adjustment at the RV center. "Ain't but a minor thing," he said, dashing out the door and promising to empty the gray water tank on his way back, which he forgot to do. For you hotelers, gray water is the used sink and shower water. Our gray water tank was near full from all of my cleaning, but we could empty it just as easily at one of the campgrounds along the way. No big deal...I thought.

Originally, our scheduled departure was to be bright and early at seven....and by three that afternoon we were all getting a bit crabby as we were still in our driveway waiting for "the launch." Finally, the trailer arrived back at our home and was, this time, "properly equipped" with the right hitching gear. We were ready to set sail...wait...that's another story.

Our sturdy vehicle was now ready to tow its new best friend, our recently remodeled camper, across the country. I might mention here that it was June, one of the hottest Junes on record, when we decided to travel three-thousand miles in a vehicle without air conditioning. Those poor pioneers! We just don't give them enough credit!

Because we left so late in the day, we barely made it across the Kansas state line. Hardly impressive, I know. But hey, it was at least over the Colorado border and it was dark when we arrived at our first campground, which made us feel like we'd traveled even farther.

Next morning, I sipped my first on-the-road cup of coffee that was made in our new camper. I looked around at a whole lot of nothing. Gosh, there really isn't much to look at in Kansas. I did think the grass was pretty, glistening in the sunshine...but one can only watch grass for so long. I remembered my best friend telling me about all of their endless drives through Kansas every summer. Now I wish I had been more sympathetic toward her.

Breakfast was cleaned up and the dishes were washed and put away (what other time is it fun to clean a kitchen than on the road in your new camper, right?)

My husband asked me if I wanted to drive for a while. I thought about it for a moment and decided I would. After all, it's only Kansas. No hills to freak me out or worry about. "Sure," I'd said...ignorantly.

A half hour down the road, I showed off my vast trailering abilities. My husband was impressed and certain that I was handling "the rig" quite well. Why, when we get on the open road, do people suddenly start sounding like truckers? I think everyone does this. Can you *Ten-Four* that, good buddy? Yes, I admit, we had a C.B. radio for our "rig."

After another twenty miles of grass and hearty cows, my husband decided to retrieve the C.B. radio from the back of the Blazer and hook it up while I was driving. Good idea, I thought. That'll give him something to do. The girls were busy playing with their road toys and seemingly entertained by them.

My husband straddled his way over seats, pillows, and toys to the "wayback" of the Blazer. In the rear view mirror I spotted his butt swinging high in the air as he dangled over the back seat reaching for the C.B. Suddenly, I found myself driving down the ONLY hill in Kansas. Yes, an impressive hill at that. A steep descent for sure! And it was at this time that a tandem semi truck briskly passed us, which caused our "rig" to go askew on the highway. The Blazer was moving left and the trailer was careening right and then they'd switch places. Yeah, real scary stuff, especially on a sudden downhill!

Earlier, we had noticed that some of the semis that had passed us did cause some mild wiggling between Blazer and trailer, but not as bad until this particular moment on the downhill! The momentum of the hill quickly escalated the hazard. Panicked, I could feel I was losing control of the Blazer...we were shooting left and the trailer was jerking right and vice versa. Yes, we were about to lose it all over a Kansas highway and my pretty new curtains would soon serve as flags to mark our pathetic remains.

In the mirror planted above my forehead, I saw my life pass before me (I really did) along with my husband's butt flying around the cabin of the Blazer. He tried to steady himself by grabbing on to anything he could grasp, but he was being bounced around, narrowly dodging my kids' heads in flight. He yelled, "Hit the trailer brakes!"

"CRAP!" I shouted. "I can't reach them!" (I didn't check this out earlier? BEFORE I started to drive the beast down the highway?)

We were really getting yanked all over the three-lane highway with a downward push. People were scrambling out of our way...I could see the terror in their faces...unless it was my own reflection in the windows. Finally, my husband made a heroic dive toward the trailer brakes and pressed mightily, which brought everything back under control.

By the time I got the Blazer back in sync with the trailer, I spotted a rest stop ahead. When I pulled in, I was shaking violently (honestly, I shook for two days after that.) My "rigging" days were over and I didn't mind.

God bless the trucker who followed us into the rest stop. He saw what had happened and offered an explanation and solid solution to our problem. He kindly explained that our hitch was installed improperly. *Grrrr...*Back to that damn hitch! The trucker also told us of a place about a hundred miles down the road where we could go for repair. For those next hundred miles, every time a semi truck passed us, our nerves grew more brittle and I know I saw three gray hairs sprout from my beloved's head.

After the "proper" hitch was installed *again*, we were back on the road with restored confidence.

To save time that day, we didn't make our lunch inside our camper as planned. We opted for a Taco Bell somewhere in Missouri. Thinking my husband would choose the sensible option to park our small house in the outer perimeter of the large parking lot, he chose the drive-thru. "Really? The drive-thru?" I firmly protested as I'm always the wise and cautious one in this family (okay, except for the trailer brake incident).

Confidently, my husband said, "Oh, yeah. This is nothing. I can pull this thing through a donut."

I gave him the stink-eye to which he resisted and followed through with his brilliant idea.

Nervously, I squirmed in my seat beside him, watching up, down, sideways left and sideways right. The small gap inside the drive-thru was rapidly getting smaller inside the curved curb. No, it wasn't my imagination; our trailer was swallowing up the void...quickly.

Suddenly, I saw that look on my husband's face. The look I most hate. It's the moment where he realizes he just screwed up. Yeah, I've seen that look a lot, I'm sure you can now sympathize with me.

Quietly, I sat in my seat...making not a peep. Instinctively, my kids knew to follow my lead. My husband continued to maneuver the watermelon through the buttonhole while we all waited for that *oops* moment. Praying, I held my breath and just when I was about to have the audacity to think we were going to make it, I heard the dreaded *CLUNK!* Promptly followed by a *THUNK!*

Immediately, I saw my husband's eyes shift in all possible directions. And that's when it hit us. A foul, slow green vapor came up through the open windows and shrouded us with its evil stench inside the hot Blazer. There was no escape from the enigma that was sucking the breath right out of us. I glared at that man sitting beside me in the Blazer and demanded some sort of explanation.

At first he offered nothing and as my gagging continued, he vehemently denied any kind of involvement with the odor. (I've since grown wise to this man after thirty years of marriage).

The gagfest continued...we suffered severely as there was no escape from our hell. Cars were in front of us and cars were lined up behind us. We were stuck.

And then, all of a sudden, a small black sports car fiercely revved his engine from behind us and squealed out of his spot and drove up and over the curb onto the pretty grassy area with flowers and bushes to make his getaway.

Ignorantly, I looked at my husband with my nose still tucked inside my shirt, believing him that we had nothing to do with the fetid air. I managed, through small wisps of air, to ask, "What's his problem? It's not our fault that Taco Bell's sewage system is having issues. Sheesh!"

My husband abandoned his conscience and only nodded in agreement.

We ordered our lunch and endured the dirty looks from the window operator who grabbed our money and threw our tacos at us before slamming her window closed. At this point, I knew something was amiss...but my self-preservation instinct, in the form of denial, kicked in.

With my lunch in my lap, I couldn't eat it. The odor had stolen my once ravenous appetite and, combined with the Missouri heat and humidity, I felt overly nauseated. I placed my mangled tacos on the console beside me and sucked in fresh air down the highway.

It was later that night, after the kids had fallen asleep in their bed above ours, that my beloved and I lay exhausted in udder darkness when he confessed to knocking the cap off of the gray water tank in the drive-thru.

And even more unsettling...I still had over two thousand miles to travel with that man.

Written by Aspen Michaels

HANGING OUT AT THE WATER PARK

It was the first week of summer break when my friends and I purchased our first bikinis...a daring maneuver that was not sanctioned by our mothers. To show off our new, colorful attire, we decided to go hang out at the local water park for the day, which featured several new water slides.

Standing guard at a particular slide was a really "hot" lifeguard. Being the boy-crazed girls that we were, of course we chose his slide. We giggled all the way to the very top of the slide only to look down at our beloved hunk trading posts with another lifeguard—a girl! We were disenchanted, to say the least. He was the only reason we were going on the massive slide in the first place.

Quickly, I assessed the enormity of the slide and considered my odds of surviving the colossal beast. Without that gorgeous lifeguard waiting down below, suddenly the risks didn't seem worth it to me anymore. My instincts warned me to avoid the slide, but my friends insisted. Deep in deliberation, I again pondered the risks before giving in to their ambition.

I ignored the persistent warning inside my head and forced myself into proper position on the slide…clearly dismissing any remains of caution. I gave myself a little push and was instantly tossed into a rushing stream of water. It was so cold that I think I shrunk a little. Halfway down this vertical jet-propelled river, I was stricken with an unfamiliar pain. An intense wedgie had formed. This, I actually anticipated, but it worsened with my increasing speed on the hundred-mile slide. I had become one with the bathing suit.

A moment later, my friends witnessed my graceless ejection from the waterslide where I was thrust into a pool...a very shallow pool, but I felt as though I were drowning in ten feet of water. Disoriented, I tumbled around looking for up and when I finally found up, I shot out of the water gasping for air. I sucked in a few dry breaths of oxygen and suddenly became conscious of my awkward state.

The uncomfortable sensations returning in my southern region reminded me of the substantial wedgie I had acquired during my hellish descent. My swimsuit had to be surgically removed....okay, I'm exaggerating slightly, but not much. Very discreetly I remedied my situation.

When I decided that I was right with the world again, I quickly surveyed the pool and its outer banks to see if anyone had played witness to my indelicate emergence. Suddenly, I caught sight of my friends laughing hysterically and pointing at me. Apparently, they saw my mishap and, apparently, I wasn't as discreet as I thought when performing my near-surgical procedure to recover my bathing suit from the far recesses of my being. I dismissed their laughter and worked myself across the crowded pool to join them. On my way over, I stole a glimpse of the "hot" lifeguard and flashed a quick smile. He had sunglasses on, but I knew he was looking right at me. I was thrilled—my vanity taking hold of me. I had won his favor, I thought smugly to myself, basking in his glances of me.

The lifeguard donned a peculiar expression and I swiftly responded with a flirty grin as I continued my passage toward my friends who were still carrying on and pointing at me.

As I got closer to them, their words finally became intelligible. A startling crash of realization nearly knocked me over when I looked down over my body and discovered that all of the crucial portions of my chest were completely exposed! Yep, there I was, just hanging out all over.

My body turned to mush as grave humiliation washed over me, hurling a portion of humble pie at me. I plunged down into the water so fast that I nearly injected water into my brain by way of my nose. I was thoroughly embarrassed as I struggled to put my top back into position under the water. I didn't want to come up out of the water...ever. And I certainly didn't want to see that lifeguard again. He had already seen plenty of me and so did my friends as well as a few hundred spectators.

I was lost inside my nightmare; woozy and drunk with embarrassment. I couldn't think of anything except strangling my friends for not attempting to get that all-important message across to me any sooner! I struggled to pull myself together as I made my way to the exit slope of the pool.

I gathered my pride, my dignity...what dignity? For a few moments I wallowed in self-pity over a cold soda until my youthful spirit returned, providing me a full recovery of the incident.

Would you believe I went down that slide six more times?

Written by Sydney Woodside

LAS VEGAS OR BLUSH

My husband and I had spent months dreaming and saving for our first trip to Las Vegas. It was a glamorous playground for grownups where parents could relax and forget about lost library books, report cards, and cat puke. We couldn't wait to indulge in our long-awaited fantasy that would briefly take us away from our simple lives.

Our fantasy began with us driving into Vegas on fumes, which sent me into a mild state of panic and quiet thoughts of murder.

My husband's tone of voice revealed his own private thoughts—*Crap!* Trekking through miles of open desert for a can of gas was not his main concern; dealing with me later over the quickly evaporating fuel tank was the issue troubling him most.

We turned off the air conditioner hoping to stretch our remaining tablespoons of gasoline while making our way through the endless desert. The menacing fuel gauge continued to mock us as we drove down the sweltering ribbon of highway. We prayed over every mile our nearly barren tank would allow while the searing winds slapped our faces.

Finally, the precious fumes that miraculously carried us through the desert were exhausted just as we pulled into the first available gas station. My husband would live, I decided.

Our fourteen-hour drive through hell ended when we arrived at the beautiful and stylish Harrah's Hotel & Casino. Our nerves were frayed, but we were determined to have fun. Forgiveness was in order, I resolved.

At the check-in desk, inside the luxurious lobby, I was immediately stricken with a disturbing revelation; people all around us were handsomely dressed and sparkling with elegance and diamonds. Pleasant fragrances from fine perfumes trickled past my nose and gleaming fixtures surrounded us; all defining a glaring imbalance that became evident when my eyes landed on my husband. Innocently, he stood at the concierge's desk in his comfortable driving attire, which consisted of a faded novelty t-shirt, scuffed blue jeans and ratty tennis shoes that even a vagrant would refuse. This fine ensemble was accessorized with a dingy baseball cap. I then caught my own reflection embedded in a plate of brass beneath a sophisticated painting. I was mortified! I had what appeared to be bed-head, road grunge and misplaced travel munchies scattered about my exterior! I wanted to climb under my wheelchair before anyone had noticed me and the other Colorado bumpkin who had just rolled in off the dirty highway.

Normally, I'm not a vain person, but our state of arrival had quickly become uncomfortable. I felt as though all eyes were upon us. Desperately, I wished the tidy man, with all of his questions, would hurry up and hand over the room key so I could vanish.

A few minutes later, we settled into our hotel room where I began to recover...and I was speaking to my husband again.

A quick visit to the pricey, yet necessary, pay-per-grab refrigerator perked me up. A shot of Jim Beam diluted with some 7-Up put us both back on track. I pulled out my nice clothes from my suitcase, showered and fixed myself up enough to do some damage control....I hoped. Redemption was in order; we could now go face our public.

An hour later, we channeled through several tables of gaming and tried our hand at a few. We pulled some arms on the bandits and finally found a section of the casino where we were more comfortable with our kind of people. It was called the Party Pit; a whimsical and informal room designed for lower stakes gambling and less intense players. I quickly forgot about the image I was trying to create for myself and realized I was there to have fun. I was me and glad to be. Well, for a while I was.

In the Party Pit, we discovered that they played a game called Red Dog. Many times we'd played this game with our poker friends. We loved that crazy game and were thrilled to find a table that actually played it. Unfortunately, the table was full so we meandered through the crowd of people until we found the only empty table in the room. This tabled played the childhood card game of WAR. It was silly, but we were eager to play anything at that point.

The dealer was devastatingly handsome and a sweetheart as well. My husband and I were his only players and he seemed to enjoy our company. We amused ourselves with several hands of WAR and conversation with him while waiting for a slot to open up at the Red Dog table.

At first, when we won a game, the WAR dealer would give me a plastic beaded necklace along with my winnings, adding to the whimsical nature of the Party Pit. After mentioning to the dealer that we had two young daughters at home, he started giving the necklaces to me even when we lost.

Finally, the Red Dog table was open for new players so my husband and I quickly bid farewell to the jovial dealer, collected our winnings, club cards, and necklaces before hurrying over to the other table only to find there was just enough room for one new player.

Knowing how much my husband loved Red Dog, I offered the slot to him and watched for a while until I became bored. I looked over toward our friendly dealer whom we'd spent so much time with and decided to rejoin him at his lonely table of WAR.

Through the lively crowd of people I made my way back to his table and, like a seasoned pro, I flashed a grin and confidently slapped my lucky club card down onto the table in front of him.

The handsome dealer just stood there on his platform looking back at me with a smoldering grin on his rugged face. So, I just sat there in my wheelchair smiling back at him, waiting for him to shuffle his cards. Then he bent over and leaned in toward me to tell me something discreetly, "I'm sorry, Ma'am, but we're not allowed to visit our guests in their hotel rooms."

Of course I didn't hear him the first time, I had to ask him to repeat it! His words ricocheted inside my brain as I tried to form a sensible reply. Panic came in pounding waves alternating with supreme humiliation. I looked down at the table and realized that I hadn't given him my club card at all, rather it was my HOTEL ROOM KEY! Blast this new technology.

I was horrified. I tried to explain that I thought I had given him my club card and that I didn't mean to give him *that* card. "They look so much alike," I pleaded in my best defense. My cheeks were inflamed with embarrassment. The more I tried to convince him of my blunder, the more my cheeks burned. I swear I saw my crimson face reflecting in his name tag. I felt lightheaded. The room was roaring and so were my ears.

By now, my own defense sounded phony even to me. I tried so hard to undo what I had done. I wanted to die. Death was my only way out, I knew, but I couldn't die fast enough! Shakespeare's famous line, "Me thinks thou doth protest too much," burned inside my head adding to my plight. Is he thinking the same thing, I wondered.

The dealer chuckled as I struggled to produce my club card quickly. I wanted my adorable husband to rescue me, but he was buried in a sea of gamblers, completely oblivious to my scandalous proposition.

The incident seemed so planned, so orchestrated! He probably thought that I mistook his kindness of earlier as flirtatious. An invitation!

Suddenly, I was aware of other sets of eyes above me as I squirmed inside my humiliation. I looked up and noticed the security bubble planted in the ceiling. On the other side of that black ball were even more observers to my outrageous proposition and subsequent rejection.

Written by Kim Vantrease

LEMONADE

Throughout my life, my mom went on and on, "Don't drink out of the same cup as others." Germs, germs! With everything, it was germs! After years of this conditioning, I was literally terrified to drink from someone else's cup. So, one hot summer day, my mom and I were driving past the little neighbor boys down the road. They were holding up a sign that read, "ICE COLD LEMONADE AND POPSICLES."

My mom said, "Oh, we've gotta buy something from them. I like to encourage young entrepreneurs."

This was the third time we'd bought from these particular entrepreneurs and the tradition went on to dump the merchandise as soon as we were out of their sight as we were concerned by the practices and cleanliness of little kids.

So, the young businessmen ran up to our car window with dollar signs flashing in their eyes.

My mom asked, "How much are your popsicles?"

The sign clearly stated they were fifty cents.

The older boy piped up, "Seventy-five cents."

I laughed inside and opted for the lemonade, not realizing at the time that my mom's strategic maneuver included choosing the completely sealed product. Meanwhile, on the other side of our car, I was busy making plans to make a successful dump of my "tainted" lemonade.

The younger boy ran to his lemonade stand and proudly poured the lemonade and brought it back to me. I set the possibly "contaminated" lemonade beside me in the cup holder as he went to retrieve my mom's popsicle.

Upon returning, the younger boy said, "Oh, and could you please drink the lemonade here? We are running short on cups."

Gulp! I looked down at the huge red 16-ounser. "Sure," I said, weakly, casting a pitiful look toward my mom who was holding back hysterical laughter. She offered no support.

Again, I looked down at the poison and slowly picked it up. I proceeded to swallow the warm, unsweetened "Ice Cold Lemonade." I put on my best fake smile, probably my last, and handed the cup back to the waiting child.

We pulled away and my mom burst out laughing so hard that she had to pull the car over. I thought she'd lose it right there. Not only did I have to drink it all, but I had to drink it from a cup that had surely been shared by all of my neighbors! Thus, the end of my lemonade stand purchases and support of young entrepreneurs.

Written by Amanda Dougherty

DEATH BY SOUP

Making my delicious potato soup on Sunday for the big snow storm...

The steam from the simmering concoction beckoned the family over to the stove. Chattering about life and watching me cook, they all bore witness to my failed attempt at mass murder.

I opened the new package of bacon pieces and shook some of its contents into the boiling promise of satisfaction, when, much to my surprise, the tiny blue dehydrating packet that declares boldly "DO NOT EAT" leaped from the bag and into my soup!

Immediately, the kitchen erupted into fierce accusations of murder plots and poisonings! All the while I was two-fisting slotted spoons, desperately searching for the blister-pack of certain death!

It was a terrific little swimmer and evaded the holy spoons with agile efficiency. But with my ninja skills and fear of murder charges looming heavily, I captured the suicidal packeteer and saved my entire family!

Although, convincing them that I was innocent from the beginning is an ongoing battle.

Written by Maile McCurry

OPEN MOUTH, INSERT BOOTS OF
ESCAPING

I was wiping down the front counter, singing
along with whatever stupid pop song was on the
radio, when the new guy walked in. He looked
normal enough, tall and bald with glasses and
smiling as he introduced himself.

I shook his hand and began showing him around the tiny square chamber that would quickly become his new home away from home. "This is the cash register, this is the grill, this is where we keep the booze. When people want something to eat or drink, write it down here, take their money, and make sure you get their lane number. Pretty simple, really."

People don't typically do a whole lot of bowling at three on a Monday afternoon, and you can only stack Styrofoam cups so high before they topple over, alas, we had some time to kill before the evening rush began. I sat on a stool near the counter and lit a cigarette (though not too close to the counter, as there are certain standards of cleanliness that must be maintained in a bowling alley snack bar).

New Guy broke out a tattered paperback and turned to a page somewhere in the middle marked by some sort of odd-looking playing card. I gave him a few minutes; you know, just long enough to start really getting into the story, when I proceeded to ask, "Whatcha readin'?"

"Oh, it's called…I can't remember the title by you've probably never heard of him. It's a Sci-Fi/fantasy type thing. This is the twelfth time I've read it. I'm kind of a nerd."

"Oh, cool," is what I replied with as I searched for some other way to connect and keep up the conversation. "Well, hey, at least you don't play Dungeons and Dragons," was the best I could do on such short notice. Genius, I know.

His response? "Um...actually, I do..."

A normal, not-awkward person would stop there, maybe even attempt to backtrack so as to avoid offending this new person that they would most likely be spending a great deal of time with in the coming months. Is that what I did? Nope. "Okay...well...at least you're not one of those guys that plays dress-up and pretends to hit each other with swords in the city park every Sunday. Am I right?" (Insert awkward laugh here.)

"Well...actually...I do that, too."

"Oh. Sorry. I'm an idiot."

"It's okay. A lot of people are."

Surprisingly, in spite of (or maybe because of?) my insensitivity, New Guy and I turned out to be pretty good work pals.

Unsurprisingly, people that work in bowling alley snack bars tend to have a decent sense of humor. How else does one cope with a barrage of drunk old men blowing smoke in one's face while describing in detail how to perfectly salt their jumbo pretzel and pour their beer without too much foam?

I learned a lot from that experience. Namely, not to make an arse out of myself by making assumptions about someone I've never met. I also learned more about D&D than I ever would have thought necessary. Turns out it's pretty much the same as fantasy football. They're both predominantly played by men. They both require countless hours of pretend play. Just swap out "your mom" for "thy matriarch" and they pretty much become interchangeable.

I even went out and watched a little LARP in the park once. Believe it or not, it was way more entertaining than any football game I've ever attended. Now if only they had tailgate parties...

Written by Kyla Hinton

Birthday Clown

We had settled in Visalia, California, a four-and-a-half-hour drive from my family in San Diego. Now in our fifties, my husband and I enjoyed time with our "second family" in a Community Bible Church. Attending the same church was our charming friend, Margaret. Widowed and living on her own, Margaret was turning eighty-four that day. Her children lived far away and couldn't make it, so we stepped in and took her out for lunch.

"Hurry, hurry, she's waiting for us," my husband commanded.

"You know I have to put my make-up on. You told her two," I replied.

"I'll warm up the car and pick her up first."

"No, give me five minutes; can't you do that for me?"

"Well, all right. I'll be in the car," he conceded.

Picking up my purse and pulling out my make-up bag, I took off my glasses and quickly took out my eyebrow pencil, lipstick liner and mascara as I had done hundreds of times before. I could put my make-up on with my eyes closed; I knew my face so well.

"OK, let's go," I said, getting in the car.

He drove to our new friend, Margaret's house. We decided to take her for a nice birthday lunch at our favorite all-you-can-eat buffet.

"Here, Margaret; I will get in the back and you ride up front where you can see better," I suggested.

"So nice of you young people to invite me," she beamed.

My husband and I glanced at each other and smiled. Not very often do you get called "young" in your fifties.

"Here we are, Margaret. Let me get your door," my husband offered.

"You two pick out a table, I have to visit the lady's room," Margaret said over her shoulder.

While Margaret was away, the waitress came to the table. She recognized my husband and he asked her to sit and chat a minute. After an energetic reunion, she turned to greet me.

Silence. She stared in my eyes. She finally mumbled and asked if we wanted something to drink. Without another word to me, she watched my face as she stood up and walked away.

"I must have spinach in my teeth, the way she looked at me."

"Here comes Margaret. You should go up there and help with her plate," my husband kindly suggested.

I met up with Margaret as I filled our tray with plates and forks. Side by side, we went around every food station, from the prime rib to the carrot cake.

People turned around and watched the two of us with smiles on their faces. Margaret was telling me an amusing story about her great granddaughter and I laughed along with her. Amazingly, several of the people around us started laughing and pointing at us. It was contagious. We smiled at each other, realizing the joy we had brought into other people's lives. Even my husband noticed our ability to entertain strangers and came to join us.

"You need to take Margaret to the lady's room. She has a problem," he urged.

"But, I…I…"

"No, I said right NOW!"

"OK. Margaret, he wants us to go to the lady's room again. Maybe he has a surprise for us."

As I turned to follow her, I was aghast…the back of her dress was tucked firmly into her pantyhose! And I had just paraded her around the entire food carousel, making sure to hit every food station from the prime rib to the carrot cake!

Fortunately, Margaret decided to try to "go" again while she was in the lady's room so I never had to explain the incident to her. I was relieved that her dignity remained intact, well sort of. At least she didn't know that her fanny had just made a special debut in the food line.

While in the restroom, I decided to check my make-up. As I looked at my eyes, I gasped in horror! Apparently, in my hurry to leave the house, I had inadvertently colored my eyebrows with my bright red lip liner instead of my eyebrow pencil!

I could only laugh at myself as there was nothing else I could do. It did strike me odd how my husband missed it though. I could expect that from an eighty-four-year old woman, but my husband? It then occurred to me, the waitress certainly noticed!

Well, happy birthday, Margaret. You even had a clown!

Written by Lynda Elliott Goyzueta

GPS ADVENTURES

A few years ago I decided it was finally time to move into the 21st century and buy a GPS unit for my car. Although I always know where I'm going, my car has issues at times. I had been thinking about buying a GPS for a while, but I procrastinated about making the purchase. I guess I could blame it on my fear that I would have trouble finding my way to a store that sold them. The purchase was easy since stores seem to love taking money for products, (I'm trying to help fix the economy) and the learning curve on using my new "personal travel assistant" promised to be brief.

The first experience with my new buddy, "Mr. GPS," went very well as I found the gas station two miles away that I've gone to for years with no trouble at all. The next day my wife and I were able to effortlessly navigate to my mother's house for Easter, and it was clear that "GPS" and I had formed a lasting relationship.

A few weeks later as my wife and I were preparing to drive to a banquet, I pulled my buddy "G" out of the box and punched in the address for a posh hotel in a nearby city...mainly because that's where we needed to go for the banquet. How comforting to look at "G's" screen and see the words, "NO MATCHES FOUND." (OK, "Mr. GPS," it's a little early in the relationship to start playing practical jokes!) A second try did provide the directions, so "GPS" must have wised up and sensed that he had crossed the line momentarily.

Our drive to the city was pretty much uneventful...until events started happening. The first turn was right on (although it was a left turn) when "G" said, "turn left and then turn right."

OK, the left was fine, but immediately turning right would have placed me squarely in the front window of an office building. Since I didn't agree with "G," I kept driving straight ahead. I noticed "GP" becoming irritated as he then insisted that I turn left. I didn't agree with that either, so I continued on without turning. Now, "GPS" was copping an attitude when he said, "Turn right—TURN RIGHT!"

(OK, "MR. GPS," how about lightening up just a little?!?) That turn put us behind a bus, which made the relevant street signs no longer visible to us, something that is always a comfort when you think you're LOST.

Well, "MR. GPS" was immediately at it again—"TURN RIGHT—TURN RIGHT!!" (You know that I can turn off your power any time I want to, don't you?) I dutifully TURNED RIGHT—TURNED RIGHT, then "Mr. GPS" proudly, and somewhat smugly, announced that we were arriving at our destination on the left.

After the banquet we gave "Mr. GPS" another chance, and he promptly advised us five minutes into the trip home to keep going on the route we were already traveling…a route we had to figure out for ourselves because of the minor technicality of satellite reception being wiped out in parking garages and when surrounded by tall buildings.

Fortunately, the uneventful ride home allowed me to calm down and abandon my original plan of introducing "Mr. GPS" to "MR. SLEDGEHAMMER."

Written by Daryl R. Clair

ON THE FLIPSIDE

Let me start out by saying that I am not a very exciting individual. Do things get a bit boring in my life sometimes? Absolutely, but I

47

don't mind. I actually like the quiet. I discovered a long time ago that the peace only found in solitude is what helps me actually get things done in my life. Sure, I get distracted with video games and other things of the sort, but, for the most part, I'm fairly productive when left to my own devices.

We're gonna call this the "heads" side of the coin.

Let me tell you the one thing I've learned in life is that there are always other sides to the proverbial coins we find generously scattered throughout our lives.

And on the "tails" side of this coin—the flipside—the times I'm not all by myself toiling away on some secret project are times filled with many many friends that can be the most…hmmm…I would like to say "interesting." But that would be a vast understatement. Another word could be "troublesome." But that might have a bit too much of a harsh bite to it. I'm gonna settle on "distracting." Yes. My friends can be very distracting. But I guess another word I could definitely use is this: exciting.

Please, allow me to tell you what happened in Texas one time. I promise a story full of moments where I had to toss that allegoric coin up in the air and only hope for the best. It was also a day I had an epiphany. I learned something important, at least to me. I learned that no matter what side that coin lands on, everything always seems to work out in the end—well, kind of…

It began, as it always does, with my cellphone going off. It was vibrating in one of the pockets of my cargo pants, sending a buzzing wave into the audio atmosphere of my meager apartment. I was sleeping heavily so a few moments passed before I was roused awake by the slight tingling sensation poking at the side of my leg. Without sitting up, I pulled the droning phone out of my pocket and answered it. I didn't have to look at the screen to know who it was— it was Tim Donnelly. He was the only person who would call me this early on a Saturday, and not because he was an early bird or anything like that. He simply was just in a later time zone than me.

"Why didn't you just text me?" were the first words out of my mouth. They sounded groggy and rough, and a little terser than I had meant.

"Because, believe it or not, Joe, people still talk to one another, you know with their mouths," Tim said. "And besides, you never even respond to your texts."

That was true. It's one of those spinning contradictions that govern my life. I don't like talking on the phone at all. I prefer my information given to me in short, little blurbs that could be absorbed quickly. But I rarely ever return a text unless it is a direct question. And even then I've been known to ignore the sender entirely until the next day.

"You're lucky I answered at all," I said to Tim and then read the time on the digital clock that was placed on my dresser. It read 6:55 in bright green numbers of segmented light. "You know it's not even seven here yet."

"You have to answer my calls. I'm kind of like your boss these days, just to inform you," Tim said.

"Ha!" I scoffed. I was starting to feel a bit more awake now, and my sarcastic side was coming out in full force. "I'm afraid you're far too old and far too slow to be my boss, Tim."

"Well, I'm the old guy who got you a race with fifteen hundred dollars awaiting the rider who makes it over the line first, and, of course, I will get my ten percent as usual."

A race! The notion intrigued me. I had only just started jumping back on the bike after the accident that had left me with a pretty bad knee. But I was better now. I even stretched my leg out, right then and there, while I was lying on my couch. I didn't feel any twinge of pain or soreness. It was like new. I could race for sure.

But before I said yes, I had a few questions.
"When is it?" I asked.

"It's the day after tomorrow. I already gotcha a top-of-the-line bike you can ride."

"Monday!" I practically shouted. "That doesn't leave a lot of time for training does it?"

"Training..." It was Tim's turn to scoff at me, "Like you need to train to beat some sea-levelers.

He was referring to the fact that I live and train in Colorado—one of the highest elevated states in the nation. Our lungs have gotten used to the lack of oxygen here, only making our stamina stronger in a place that is at sea level, where the air seems nearly endless.

"I don't know, man," I said. I was just messing with Tim now, how I like to do sometimes, making life a little hard for the guy who has had everything so easily handed to him. "I don't race anymore. I just write about it now. Think of me like a desk jockey in the mountain-biking world."

"C'mon man, you know what I had to do to get you on that starting linc."

"I hope, for your sake, some graphic sexual acts," I said and snickered a little.

"Don't be stupid, nothing like that. I pulled some clout with some people I know and laid down the entrance fee for ya. So you have to do it."

"I'm just messin' with you, man. I'll do it," I said. "How did you get me in so fast, though? What people do you know out there?"

"The guy who dropped out of the race is the brother of the bride in the wedding I'm going to be the best man in tomorrow. Is that confusing enough for ya?"

"I stopped listening after you said 'the.'"

"Yeah, that's what I figured. Anyways, I already scheduled you a flight that leaves D.I.A. tomorrow morning at eight fifteen. I'll pick you up from the airport and we'll drive back to the hotel. You can chill there until after the wedding. Sound cool?"

"Yep. Looks like it's gonna be another early morning tomorrow."

Now, I know what you're thinking. You probably think that this is a story about how I struggled and eventually overcame some type of inner problem and won the race. I'm sorry to mislead you, but you would be wrong in that assumption. I did indeed go to the race and crossed the line in third place, taking home seven hundred dollars, minus the ten percent promised to Tim, even though I can't believe he accepted it after what happened. But the race is not what this tale is about. It is about what happened right after I stepped off the plane in Texas. That was when things got out of hand. But maybe a better way to put it is, crazy.

I stepped out of the airport and onto the sidewalk that lined the area where pick-ups are made. I pulled my phone out and thumbed for Tim's number. He had said to call when I had landed, so when I found his number I pressed the send button. The phone rang. And then rang again. No answer.

Damn it, I thought. I was getting nervous. This was just what I needed right now, to be stranded in the middle of Texas—the largest state in America.

I dialed Tim's number again and waited. The air was hot here and a little more humid than in Colorado. And I felt moisture instantly cling to my forehead and neck. I could see other people being picked up by their loved ones and friends. They all smiled and hugged each other upon meeting. Then they would pile their suitcases and backpacks into their cars and trucks before driving away. I remember thinking that when I saw Tim he wasn't going to get a hug; he was going to get a punch in the stomach. Just as I thought this, he finally answered.

"Are you here?" he asked. He sounded frantic and upset.

"Yeah, I just stepped off the plane. I'm waiting outside. Are you here?"

"I see you. Pulling up right beside you."

Sure enough, as I looked up, I saw him behind the wheel of a small white pick-up truck. He stopped a foot away from me. I felt a flood of relief. At least I wasn't going to end up stranded at the airport. I ended the call and got closer.

"What's up?" I said, looking at him through the open window. I was right, he was in a tussle. He seemed real frantic. He was soaked in sweat, which reeked of booze, and his salt-and-pepper colored hair was matted to his face in long, stringy clumps. I threw my bag in the bed of the truck—I always travel light—and then I opened the passenger-side door and stepped in.

"We're in trouble," is the only thing Tim said and then we drove off.

On the way to the groom's house, which was almost an hour away, Tim filled me in on what was happening. He told me he had lost the wedding ring that he had been asked to hold onto by the groom. It had been in his coat pocket. But when he woke up this morning he couldn't find the coat. He had already checked the hotel room numerous times. Then, while he was accusing one of the maids of theft, it dawned on him that he had taken his coat off when he and the groom had gone to his house before going out to a bar. He thought maybe the coat was there.

After what felt like an eternity of staring at flat, boring land, we finally made it to a residential neighborhood full of houses. He pulled in and made several turns until we were in front of the right one. The house was empty, of course, with everyone being down at the church getting ready for the ceremony.

"What time is the wedding?" I asked, looking up at the classic picture-perfect house in front of me. It looked like something from a magazine cover, complete with a white, picket fence surrounding it.

"It's at six tonight," Tim answered as he was scoping out the house as well.

I looked at the time on my phone—almost twelve. "Cool, we got plenty of time."

We got out of the truck and stepped up to the front door. Tim turned the knob but it was firmly locked shut. "Break it open," he told me.

"Screw that," I said back. "I'm not going to jail for you, bro."

I saw Tim smile for the first time since I had gotten here. "I know. I'm just kidding. Let's go around back."

We jumped a fence and checked all the windows and the patio door. They were all locked.

"Do you think they would lock the bedroom window?" I said, pointing up to a screen panel on the side of the house.

"I don't know. Here let me stand on your shoulders."

"No! Let me stand on your shoulders."

"Fine. But just know that whoever gets up there is going to have to break off the screen to check the window. And you didn't even want to break the door."

There was a moment of silence. I was thinking. I was flipping that coin.

"Alright, get on my shoulders," I said.

He did. I leaned up against the house and he grunted and climbed his way on top of my shoulders. I felt all his weight bare down on my lower back. Tim wasn't a light man.

"Hurry," I said.

After a second, I heard something crack and then the screen covering fell to the grass.

"It's open!" Tim called to me.

"That's great," I grumbled. "Can you get in?"

"Yep. I got it open wide enough that I think I can… if I…"

I felt his weight waver on top of me and I had to steady my stance to hold him. Then I felt a release from all of it. Tim was off of me. I stepped back from the house and looked up. I saw Tim hanging half-way out of the window.

His legs were randomly kicking up and down as he tried to pull himself in all the way.

"C'mon, old man. You can do it. Push! Push!" I yelled to him.

"Shut up!" Tim yelled back. "You're gonna attract attention."

"I'm gonna attract attention! You're the one with your ass hanging out of a second story window."

I heard him say something else but, I couldn't make it out. He had already pulled his body in through the window.

I watched him completely disappear into the house.

"Tim!"

He poked his head out of the window. "Stay there," he said, "I'm going to go open the patio door."

I gave him a thumbs up and waited.

When we were both inside he told me to check the living room; he said that he was going to go check the kitchen.

"What does it look like?" I asked before we parted ways.

"It's a wedding ring, what do you think it looks like?"

"Not the ring, the coat."

"It's a coat. It's a blue coat," Tim said impatiently.

57

"You don't got to get all sassy about it," I said. "What the hell are you doing with a coat here anyways? It's like a thousand degrees."

I was talking to myself by then. Tim had already gone into the kitchen.

After a few minutes of rummaging through the couch and other areas of the living room, it was apparent that what we were looking for wasn't there. I had given up and was sitting on the couch when Tim came out of the kitchen.

"Did you find it?" I asked.

"Yep," he said with a huge smile. In one hand, he had his coat. And in the other, he had a small black box. "Got it right here."

"Cool, let's go then."

That was when we heard a knock at the front door. We both stood motionless, staring at each other. Neither of us knew what to do. I slowly moved over to a window and moved the curtains over a sliver. I peered out and saw a man in a police uniform standing outside.

I turned to Tim with wide eyes. "It's the cops," I whispered.

"What?"

"It's the cops," I said again, but not any louder. Tim heard me; he just didn't want to believe it.

There was another round of knocking.

"Let's just go out the back," Tim said.

"No way, man," I said, still whispering.

"We should just tell him what's going on. Just call the groom and he'll clear everything up with the police."

More knocking pounded from the door.

"And admit that I lost his ring?"

"Who cares, you got it now."

"He will," Tim said.

We didn't have time for this. The more we waited to answer the door, the more suspicious it all looked. "Fine, let's go out the back," I said. "I'm going to jail. I just know it."

We got to the patio window and snuck a quick peek outside. There was another cop out there too. He was bent over, examining the screen that was lying in the grass.

"We're screwed," I said to myself. And I was right.

About an hour and a half later we were both sitting in a tiny holding cell at the local police-station. Our handcuffs had been removed when we arrived and then we were put into the cramped confines of grimy iron and dingy cement. I was pacing back and forth, bumping my hand into each individual bar, while Tim sat on the steel bed, silent in thought. This was jail. I had finally gone to jail—and in Texas no less.

We had tried to call the groom back at the house, but no one answered. We tried the bride, even the priest. But still we were left with only voicemails. The cops didn't believe our story at all, that's what I thought anyway when they were hauling us off and subjugating us, putting both the coat and the ring along with all our other possessions into some mysterious evidence locker that was far from Tim and I. All seemed lost. The wedding, the race, it all seemed so lost.

What was the flipside? It was hard to find one at the time, but I did. "Well," I said, "at least I can say I've gone to jail now. You know what Aristotle taught. To truly enjoy life you have to experience every little thing about it—even the bad parts."

"Don't try and be all positive right now. It's okay to admit that I messed up huge, okay."

I couldn't believe it. Tim was admitting a mistake. It didn't feel right to me.

"It's all good, man," I said and then I was surprised by Tim's sudden outburst of anger that was directed at me.

"No, it's not, alright!" Tim shouted. "You just can't keep going through life acting like you're gonna be young forever and that everything is going to be okay, because some things don't, Joe. Sometimes things end up horribly wrong."

"So what? Should I end up being an old drunk like a certain someone in this jail house?"

Tim just stared at me with daggers in his eyes. He stayed quiet—uncomfortably quiet. So I kept talking, getting louder, to the point of shouting.

"And who in the hell doesn't answer their phone on their wedding day? I mean, who is this guy." I was getting heated now; I was getting mad, as I do when I'm verbally prodded at. I had to calm down so I took a deep breath.

"I don't mean that you should be like me, and you know that," Tim said, after he let me finish my rant. His voice had more calmness to it than before. "I just mean that one day you're gonna take a fall way worse than what happened when you busted your knee. And then you won't be able to ride anymore. You know? I'm just saying you should start looking into other options."

"You're saying I should go to school, like always," I said.

"Yes, man. I've always told you to do that so that you don't end up like me."

In that moment, I flipped a symbolic coin that I had been putting off for a long damn time. Should I go to college? In that moment—behind bars in a Texas prison—I made my decision. "Alright, I'll go," I said to Tim.

"You will?" Tim said.

But before I could confirm my answer I was cut off by our arresting officer opening the jail doors.

"I want to talk with you two," the officer said.

He pulled us into a small office-like room with only a desk and a few chairs in it. The police officer sat in the chair behind the desk. He motioned for us to do the same. We did, taking our seats across from him.

"Now," he said, crossing his arms, "do you want to try your story one more time on me?" His face was stone. He had a mustache that twitched every now and then when he breathed.

I looked at the clock on the wall—it was almost five forty. It wasn't too late for the wedding. We just had to convince this man that what we were saying was the truth.

"Yes," I brazenly said, "we could try and tell you everything over again, and you could sit and listen, looking for any inconsistencies in our story, but that won't do any of us any good. And it especially won't do the bride and groom any good, which, in just twenty minutes, are ready to start their lives together." I looked at the officer's name tag. It said "Dotty." Then I looked at his hand and noticed a wedding ring. "Officer Dotty, I know you don't think we're dangerous, otherwise you wouldn't have come in here all by yourself with us. So that means you believe us just a little. Right?"

He nodded but only slightly.

"I see that you're married yourself," I continued. "Now, can you imagine something like this happening on your wedding day, and how devastating that would have been for your wife? You have to believe us and let us get that ring to the wedding."

That was it. That was all I had. If he didn't buy that then it looks like we were spending the night in jail.

"Don't worry kid. We believe you," Officer Dotty said in his heavy southern accent.

"You do?" Tim and I said in unison.

"Yeah, we called the church you said the wedding was taking place at and finally got a hold of someone. They confirmed your story."

"So why all this?" I asked, referring to the room we were in. "Why the interrogation?"

"Because," Officer Dotty said, "the church said they have never seen anyone of your description before so I just had to make sure. You can go, both of you."

After Officer Dotty told us we were free to leave, all our possessions were returned to us including the ring. Tim was elated, but we still didn't have a lot of time to get to the wedding. So the police department was kind enough to give us a ride back to the groom's house to retrieve our truck. Then they gave us a two car escort all the way to the church. I drove while Tim changed into his tuxedo.

When we arrived, we discovered that a few random cars had followed us, thinking that a president must be in the truck because of all the police cars escorting it. (I guess it doesn't take much to impress Texans).

The ceremony took place without a hitch and everything turned out fine—even with all the extra folks who showed up. I was the only one there wearing cargo shorts and a t-shirt with everyone else all decked out in their best suits and dresses.

I saw the brother who had dropped out of the race. His arm was in a thick cast. Oh, so that's why he had to drop out, I thought. I was pleased because all these little mysteries were being answered for me. Everything was coming together. Yeah, it was definitely a good time for everyone. Tim was even happy because all the drinks were free. It was the stereotypical wedding, filled with laughing, drunken dancing, and happiness.

Sometimes, while I'm sitting in class, I think back at my time with Tim in Texas. And I wonder would I still be here had we not gone to that jail cell and yelled at each other like we did.

And then I always realize it doesn't matter. Because everything worked out the way it was supposed to.

But on the flipside: Too bad I heard the bride and groom got a divorce three months later.

Written by Joseph Isaacs

STORAGE CLOSET WARS

A few months ago we experienced a Saturday that was, for the most part, one of the most perfect fall days that anyone could imagine...blue sky, not a cloud in sight, and comfortable temperatures. It was a day that practically begged you to be outside doing...anything. So, as my wife and I headed for our basement that has no windows (although I'm considering putting in a skylight) we planned to take care of the simple task of building a "portable storage closet" we had recently purchased to provide a stationary spot for clothing that's not moving around at the moment.

We were sure this task would be a breeze because the bulleted description on the box read, "EASY NO-TOOL ASSEMBLY." I didn't realize it until later, but that was apparently the manufacturer's packaging code for "this will surely be the death of you."

Everything seemed to move along smoothly at first. Within the first ten minutes, we had the plastic wrap peeled off the box and the staples removed so that we could extract and organize the pieces of the closet. Fortunately for us, the directions were written in...DIAGRAMS!!! After we had mastered the first drawing that required us to put Part I into E, (except after C) we progressed quickly through the next four steps.

Feeling a great sense of accomplishment for having been able to distinguish unlabeled, similarly sized and shaped pieces from one another, my wife and I stood back to admire our work and take a quick rest from our state of near exhaustion. Portable storage closet construction is not for the faint of heart.

There, in front of us, stood the nearly-completed portable storage closet which, for the time being, gave no indications it had plans of going anywhere. One diagram to go and we were headed outside for some fresh air. Diagram #6, or "your worst nightmare diagram," as I repeatedly referred to it while we disassembled most of what we had already done, indicated that the metal frame was supposed to have been built inside the cloth covering. (You're telling me this in the final diagram?!?) It was the equivalent of mentioning that the ship was supposed to be built inside the bottle after it was all ready to sail! Visions of camels and eyes of needles flashed before our eyes as my wife and I strained to squeeze the sixty-inch metal frame inside the zippered cloth covering that was about the size of a washcloth.

When the three-hour wrestling match with the "easy to assemble" storage closet came to an end, we had a chance to enjoy the last bit of fading sunshine as we took a walk to the end of our driveway. To the manufacturer's credit, the information on the box was correct! The storage closet was very easy to move. We had no problem transferring it from the basement to the spot where the garbage truck would pick it up early the next week.

Written by Daryl R. Clair

S.S. Burgundy

A full sized Pontiac Bonneville constructed in 1988 is approximately nineteen feet long, weighs about four-thousand pounds, and is composed of fiberglass, metal and textile. A full sized Bayline Capri boat constructed in 1988 is approximately nineteen feet long, weighs about twenty-eight hundred pounds, and is composed of fiberglass, metal and textile. The major difference between these marvels of human engineering is their buoyancy properties. I found this out the hard way.

The decade was the 00's: The year was 2005: Driving down the road at sixteen years old is the greatest experience imaginable. My grandparents had given me (in their misguided wisdom) their old Pontiac Bonneville for me to cut my teeth on. Far from a pristine automotive, the slightly used old gal would soon be a timeline of the adolescent driving experience.

The odd collection of metal was precariously held together by maroon candy colored paint punctuated by a collection of battle scars. There was the time that my brother had thrown a Frisbee a foot to the left of my waiting grasp. There was that time I drove to the movie theater and had the idea to sneak a bit of dad's liquor to my friends in the backseat. Who would have known that vomit could take the paint off of a rear fender? That nice little bruise from that one time I was mowing the lawn and hit that rather obviously placed rock. There was that house, the planter pot, that curb, the sign, that bike that one time, and all the solid objects I thought I had just missed. Yet, for all its "character," those four wheels could take me anywhere (within the town limits) and that is the greatest thing a sixteen-year old could ever hope for. Freedom.

Driving to school also became a chance to assert my dominance on the hierarchy of awkward, frustrated sex-craving teenagers. Apparently, bragging about the fact that my grandparents happened to need a new set of wheels was a testament to my own manhood. Before each flight, in an effort to sweeten my persona by a few percentage points, I would ease the driver's seat to a cool fifty degrees.

Simultaneously, I would input the only rap Compact Disc I owned (yes, it was Tupac) into my horribly self-installed Wal-Mart stereo (yes, they do sell those) and would proceed to turn the volume knob up to the "horrible distortion" level. Add to this my scratched and smudged sunglasses along with a rambunctious co-pilot amped up on coffee, hormones, violence and nicotine and you have a masterful level of both visual and auditory handicapping.

On one particular spring afternoon, I decided to escape the lectures, books and inanity of the otherwise healthy academic environment. This would not have been a deviation from a standard school day my senior year, except for the monsoon warning that was being broadcast in radio, print and television media. As an individual that didn't believe in the flawed news media system, biased towards sensationalism, I was fully unaware of these developments.

As I pulled onto Gardner Avenue, I wearily eyed the nosy old woman on the corner as she spied me through the window. She sneered at my smoking maroon monster as I started my way down the street's steep incline, loudly talking to my co-pilot as the water burbled on the blacktop. Picking up speed, I became excited by the prospect of an early nap and a bowl of cereal. Without warning, an icy splash hit the front of the car as if a tidal wave had rushed up from an angry sea. With that splash came death, swiftly administered by my father. The engine's gentle hum became a sputtering mess, struggling for air until it finally succumbed to drowning.

Floating in the bed of water, I opened the door with the intention of checking the damage under the hood. What I didn't consider, was that fact that the water level was now higher than the base of the doorframe and that water would certainly go the path of least resistance. An unstoppable hemorrhaging of water now began to turn my freedom wagon into the S.S. Burgundy, the future name that would haunt my vehicle until its eventual retirement.

In my panic, I tried to shut the door, only to be overpowered by the water's awesome force. In my struggle I heard my passenger yelling obscenities at me, angrily berating me for my terrible driving skills.

I grabbed the small wastebasket that sat on my floor, and tried to scoop out the water that was now well up to that center console thing that is only good for eating sunglasses and change. After I filled my bucket to the brim, I realized there was no possible way of making this situation work, and tossed the wastebasket into the backseat; soaking, in the process, the driest area of my upholstery. I grabbed the only thing of value in my car, my stereo, and ripped with all my might to dislodge it from the dashboard. Wires inside became twisted and broken tendons limply hanging from the soaking woodwork. Stereo in hand, I waded to the front of the car and vainly attempted to pop the hood.

As I struggled with the latch, I looked at my new surroundings. Observing the carnage, I saw a six-foot tall, mustached, slightly overweight gentleman with his arms angrily folded. I guess that driving one's car into a temporary pond is not amusing to a uniformed police officer.

In my haste to my perfect afternoon off, I had failed to realize the temporary sign erected to the left of the road warning of unfortunate events ahead. Further, I had failed to see the blue Nissan floating off to the left of the road and the flashing lights offering limited help.

Waving my now useless stereo over my boat, I looked into the simultaneously stupefied and annoyed face of a man that would soon be questioning me for two hours about my sobriety.
Written by Daniel John Bach

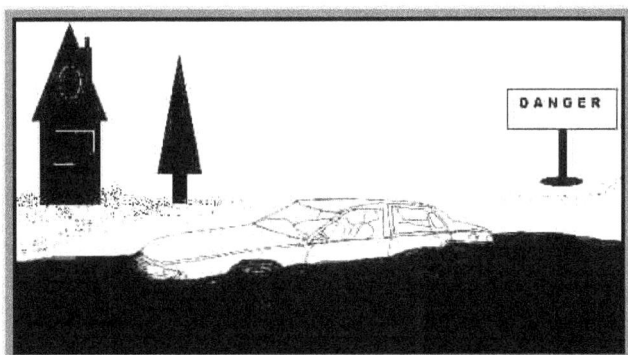

THAI ICE

I was a world traveler by the time I was seventeen. Colorful stamps from Peru, Italy, England, Russia, Mexico, Canada, Ecuador, Zimbabwe, Germany and India decorated my passport. Yet the one place that will always hold my heart is Thailand. No, not for the exotic beaches, or the elephant rides, or the sticky mango bun eating contest I shamelessly won against a rural Thai boy who had probably trained his entire young life for; but rather, the spontaneous dance moves performed by half of the Bangkok police brigade.

Let me back up a bit. For nearly two weeks, my friend and I had been wandering the small towns along the Chao Phraya River. By the time we departed our barge in the Bangkok port, we were slathered in sweat and mango bun flour. We needed a hot shower and a quick squat, more commonly known in The States as a bathroom break. Earlier, a fellow passenger on the barge had mentioned a popular temple attraction that had out-of-ground toilets; a real treat from what we had become accustomed to.

When the time came, we made our way to the temple in a little yellow TukTuk—think of a three-wheeled motorcycle, complete with canopy and a clown-car truck bed going ninety mph on the highway with thirteen passengers crammed in the back.

After arriving safely at the temple, we paid our donation for admittance and hustled through the prayer areas in search of the holy grail of toilets. There, in the far back corner of a side room, stood a door with the universal bathroom symbol. Faintly, we heard the sound of singing angels. Excitement shot through us like lightning and we could barely contain our joy.

We high-tailed it to the door and shoved against it with brute force only to be slapped in the face by a harsh wave of disappointment. The door was locked by an occupant; something we hadn't considered. The wait began. We paced, and paced, and paced. Seconds turned into minutes, minutes turned into more minutes. Our bladders were shrinking and both of us were sure the day would never come for that door to open.

Desperate, my friend cracked first. Her fist went to the door, banging loudly and she begged in her best broken Thai to please be let in. In all fairness, I think I am embellishing a bit by inserting the word, "please" here.

A woman's muffled voice yelled back through the door. Even with our ever-present knowledge that our Thai wasn't so good, we were both fairly certain that what she had said to us was something to do with "Screw Off," yet with much more vulgarity and a brief comment about our mamas.

This sent my typically placid friend into a downright assault on the door. I stood frozen as she kicked and yelled at the door. She fired off her first offense…a strong insinuation that she would take her bathroom break on the occupant's mama or otherwise.

This tantrum did not bode well with the passersby or the two temple guards within earshot of her tirade. As the two men slowly, but pointedly, made their way toward us, I quickly tried to calm my friend down and peeled her off the door. Immediately, I directed her attention toward our soon-to-be escorts who would presumably initiate our swift and, hopefully, dignified exit from the temple.

Still engulfed by rage, my friend wasn't at all concerned by their presence and she demanded again to be let into the bathroom.

Our situation didn't look promising as the two men began radioing others and, shortly thereafter, more men in dark, mean-looking uniforms showed up near the temple entrance. Through her ridiculous anger, she must have seen my face and had a similar thought as mine...our life was slowly becoming a version of the second Bridget Jones movie where she was held in a Thai prison until Darcy came to rescue her. Unfortunately, our prison would probably have less cigarettes and singing and more starvation and death.

My friend quickly began apologizing for her escapades and we started gathering our things to indicate that we would leave peacefully and that there was no need for an arrest. Two men grabbed each of us by the arm and forcibly helped us make our way to the police waiting for us just outside of the temple gates.

It must have been a slow day for crime in Bangkok because it seemed the entire police department had shown up to see what the ruckus was about. As we were gently shoved outside and into the hands of awaiting law enforcement, I impulsively yelled, "Stop!" It must have been loud, or at least louder than I had intended, because that is just what they did. They stopped. I think I startled the policeman standing beside me who was holding my backpack.

Cautiously, I looked at the officers, fear coursing through my veins and the only next thought in my head, as ridiculous as it was, "collaborate and listen…" Yes, those were the actual words that came out of my mouth.

Silence. My eyes shot to my wide-mouthed friend, shock plastered across her face. I then looked into the eyes of the policeman still holding my backpack. He had not yet decided how he was going to handle me. I was on the verge of crying or laughing; my body wasn't sure which emotion would come out first. And right as the tears began to well up in my eyes, I heard, "Ice, Ice, Baby."

It had a thick accent to it, clearly Thai. I raised my head and looked over at the group of police officers that looked younger than my little brother. They were starting to giggle and then one of them started off with, "*du, du, du, du ,du ,du.*"

My friend laughed. I laughed. The policeman holding my backpack laughed. And the dance began.

The group of young policemen began to break it down, though in a slightly muted version of the famous dance. It lasted but a minute when one of the dancers was reprimanded with a stiff smack by a senior officer. For that brief moment, I was possibly happier than I ever had been.

When the rest of the officers had pulled themselves together, they all conversed in a brief conversation, shoved our backpacks at us, and pushed us towards the bustling street that lay ahead.

My friend and I scurried down the road, surprised by our lack of shackles and flabbergasted by the events that had just unfolded. I turned to my friend and said, "Can you believe that? Vanilla Ice just saved our lives."

Written by Jill Berliner

WRONG NUMBER

My husband and I, along with our two teenaged daughters, had just moved into our new home. This new house was settled in a small town inside the Colorado foothills where we wanted to finish rearing our daughters.

I was excited about the idea of living in a small town where everyone was friendly and everybody knew everybody; it seemed so pleasant in the movies. *Aunt Bee, here I come!* I was even going to start baking pies.

Moving to the small town would get us back to a simpler life with less chaos and congestion. Hostile people would be a thing of the past as they only existed in the big cities.

It was our first Saturday night in our new place. Things weren't quite unpacked yet leaving disorder to rule my home, but not for long. So, on this particular evening, as we were breaking in our new house, we decided to order pizza from the little deli in town. You know, establish a friendly rapport with the business community right away.

After I dialed the number, I waited and then heard, "Hello?" Hmm, that's a funny way to answer a business line, I thought. But I went ahead and explained to her that I needed to place an order for a pizza. Immediately, my ear was full of angry words delivered by a sharp tongue giving me a serious lashing for misdialing!

"Oh, I'm sorry," I quickly offered, apparently too late.

When the woman got her point across, rather harshly I might add, she slammed her phone down on me, which promptly disconnected our call.

I felt my face burn with embarrassment...but then that embarrassment turned to outright rage. "How dare she holler at me like that!" I sputtered to my daughter who stood witness to my scolding. "Apparently, this *poor* woman had to endure such atrocities from others who accidentally dialed her number," I huffed.

Suddenly, I could feel myself growing stupid with rage. But did I put it into check? Of course not. I let my emotions decide my next move. A move I will forever regret.

I sat for a moment...irritated...plotting. "This woman needs to be taught a lesson," I declared boldly to my daughters who suddenly got *that* look in their eyes. They knew me too well.

"Give me that phone," I commanded in my calm (not really) state.

Reluctantly, my obedient daughter handed over the phone.

"*Hmpf*," I snorted rather sanctimoniously as I dialed, remembering to cleverly block my phone number before I launched my retort (assault) on her. After I delivered a stern moment-long lecture to the rude stranger regarding the matters of courtesy, phone etiquette and patience, I slammed my phone down on *her* this time (actually, I was only able to push the off button, but I liked to believe that the effect was just the same.)

Feeling satisfied by putting her in her place, I went about my business and successfully ordered the family pizza.

Suddenly, my phone rang. It was her bawling me out again!

Stupidly, I looked to both of my daughters, seeking some kind of explanation! I was astonished at the woman's keen wizardry. My jaw couldn't drop any closer to the floor at this point. It wasn't what she had just said to me during this next round of yelling at me, but it was how the heck did she get my phone number?

Dumbfounded, I looked at my eldest for answers, "I blocked my phone number!" I explained excitedly, "so how did this woman get our number?" I was mystified. She must have connections I quickly concluded with heavy suspicion. Serious connections. CIA? FBI? AT&T? Who was my betrayer, I wondered.

"Mom, you can't be serious," my eldest managed before falling into hysterics on the floor. Both my girls struggled to explain my blunder as they could hardly breathe from laughing.

Finally, I understood that when I originally called the woman by accident, my phone number wasn't blocked...so it was registered in her phone with my first call. I had gotten so upset, so quickly, that I'd forgotten this key element.

Cringing, I sunk in my chair, smothered in humiliation and idiocy...but mostly ashamed of the terrible example I'd made for my kids.

The moral of my story....humble thyself.

Oh, in case you're wondering…yes, a couple of times over the years, I have accidentally dialed *that* number again in hot pursuit of that troublesome pizza.

Written by Aspen Michaels

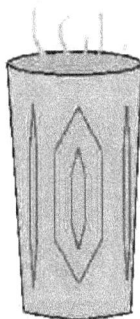

YOGIS

I don't suffer from any real issues. I try my hardest to be normal, to fit in and to never draw attention to myself. That's the important part, head down, walk fast, please don't notice me.

I have eaten the wrong meal in restaurants, I have paid more than I should have for lots of things. I have quickly apologized to people who have inconvenienced me, stepped on my toe or rudely run into me, just to make my escape quickly and unnoticed.

In coffee shops, I order what my friends and family order to avoid someone asking me a question I won't know the answer to right away. I never visit new stores, restaurants or anything that isn't a big chain with people coming in and out unnoticed.

In the spring of 2013, I decided to try something fun and different, artichoke spinach dip with cream cheese, Swiss cheese, and a simple little packet. It was pretty darn good at lunchtime.

At dinner time, which on this particular night was during my evening driving job, my tummy began to make that rumble sound that makes you feel like you should be home in the privacy of your own bathroom. The bathroom with the heavy wood door and nicely painted walls. The one with the toilet paper you like, the fan you can turn on, and the lock on the door that keeps you at least ten feet from the nearest human being. The one with the toilet brush, Comet, and handy plunger right there if you need it.

I was miles from that bathroom. I was miles and miles from that bathroom. My mom was driving with me that evening; a fun thing we do. We were nearly to our first of ten stops all over the metro area when the rumble became an urgent situation.

My dear mother got me to the nearest *7-11*; a place where I wouldn't have to ask for a bathroom key.

The door was locked...someone was inside. *Please hurry. Please.*

After several minutes I did something I would not ordinarily do to a locked bathroom door, because I so deeply respect it. I knocked. No answer. I banged. I couldn't believe it myself, but I banged on the door. And then I asked the attendant for help. His answer, "*Hmm*, he been in there while, is raining outside, hehehe."

Sir. You do not understand my situation. Quit giggling about the bathroom hogger and get me in there. I left and informed my mom that I was not in better shape. In fact, I was in worse shape.

We hopped onto the main thoroughfare, at five-thirty p.m. rush hour....and crept. And Crept.

My pants were unbuttoned and unzipped and me and my seatbelt were twisted in the seat in a way that was obvious to other motorists that I needed a restroom. Now! "Antique store, costume shop, tobacco store...carpet..."

For me, I have to purchase something in someone's place of business in order to use their restroom, even in my condition, this rule mattered. "Car parts...Come on! Where's a stupid gas station? Aha! Coffee shop! Is it open? It's open! Turn here!"

I race to the door, gather my senses, open it and am immediately standing in an espresso bar. Not a come and get your coffee and go place. An espresso bar. They are talking about coffee. They are not my kind of people, they are the kind of people my husband refers to as "Tofu Sucking Hippies." I love and respect these people, but I don't fit in. This must have been obvious to the barista, because he quickly dove into an advertisement for this coffee he was selling.

My mom always orders a Tall Decaf Mocha, no whip. That was NOT going to fly in this place. I heard Ethiopian something, Ok, when he stops talking I will order a small cup of that.

The guy at the bar turns and says, "They have a good mocha here."

YES! that's more like it. Awesome! "I will take a small mocha...and where's your restroom?"

"Around the corner and to your left."

Around the corner and to my left was a long hall. Good enough as I wouldn't be just on the other side of the door from the espresso bar.

I follow the hall and land in a room; a luxurious locker room, complete with a couch covered in silk pillows, and throws, carpet, and real vanities with real hand towels. *Crap.*

I find the toilet. The wall is barely taller than me. It's literally in the middle of the locker room and all the happy yoga ladies are standing around it. Quietly, meditation quiet. Quiet like you just yoga'd and you aren't ready to face the real world yet. I don't participate, but I know enough to know that what I was about to do, was not going to go over well in this room. But it was too late.

I did my business and with no other choice, I proudly walked out of the stall. I used the fancy vanity…I used the fancy soap and I used the fancy white hand towel.

They looked. They knew. Oh yes, they noticed me. I was not invisible in my jeans and jacket using a restroom clearly designed and marked for "Yogis." I didn't bother trying to hide. A sheepish smile as I exited would have to do.

Now we're back to the espresso bar where I had ordered something. Good, a mocha to go! I was only slightly insulted that he hadn't asked me if I wanted it to go, because I was so glad it was. He then offered to choose a coffee to take home with me as well. After what I had just done in that bathroom, I felt obligated.

Twenty-four dollars later, I made my way back to the car with a cup of mocha and a twelve-ounce bag of beans. I had never loved the inside of a car so much.

After my third visit to another restroom that evening...my mom finally mentioned a simple medicine that could have ended my troubles much sooner!

Written by Lucy Cross

DEF-CON ONE!

Like most people, I enjoy today's gadgets like answering machines to take our calls in our absence, or avoidance, whichever the case, electronic tablets, iPods, smart phones and electronic flyswatters. It's a fun time to be alive and indulge in such toys. However, these innocent-looking devices can sometimes lead to prickly situations.

On a clear and sunny morning, I sat at my desk paying bills; one of my most despised jobs as the domestic engineer. Honestly, I would rather scrub toilets.

I was already crabby and scolded myself for waiting for the last minute to pay the monthly bills. I hurried to affix the stamps to the corresponding envelopes hoping to beat the mailman to my mailbox.

My most dreaded job was nearing completion and my dark mood was beginning to lift. I could hear the birdies chirping once again in the driveway. I reached for the last bill with its accompanying envelope when I discovered that I was out of stamps. It was the most important bill of all...our mortgage! "Oh, why didn't I start with that one," I fretted, truly convinced that if I was one day late on a bill, my entire world would collapse.

I rushed to the window to check the status of the ongoing repairs to my car. I spotted my husband's feet wiggling beneath my broken down heap while vital components belonging to the engine lay scattered across the driveway. Not a good sign.

Frustration swept over me as my desperation grew. I had no way to get to the post office to buy that all important stamp to mail that stupid house payment.

My head grew hot as I cursed my procrastination and unpreparedness. I then remembered my next-door neighbor. Jubilation! She is always prepared for everything—nuclear holocaust, the plague, drought, famine; you name it, she's ready. She even has a hundred rolls of toilet paper stored in her basement.

I quickly reached for my phone hoping to catch her before she left for work. My impatient fingers dialed the phone number only to reach a wrong number in my haste. Again I dialed and was fast approaching madness as my frustration continued to fester.

My neighbor's son, a teenager, answered my telephone call. I couldn't tell if I had just woken him up or interrupted his morning routine, but he didn't sound too happy with me anyway. With teenagers though, who really knows what they are thinking?

He put the phone down and called out for his mother, stating she had a phone call.

Meanwhile, I unjustly mocked him while he was away from the phone, "Mom, the phone's for you," I repeated in the most obnoxious tone I could render. Did I mention I was in a foul mood?

Immediately, after rudely mocking him, I was shocked by my terrible behavior and berated myself inside my head. What was the matter with me? What I had considered a poor attitude on his part was only my own distorted perception due to MY personal situation. I was now really disgusted with myself for picking on an innocent kid!

Finally, my friend came to my rescue offering a stamp. Not that I deserved it now! But there was still hope; the mailman was on the other block so my grease-covered husband ran next door to retrieve the necessary stamp.

Riddled with shame, I realized what a monster I had let myself become over a very small situation. Isn't it amazing how clear things seem when you're not frustrated?

While drinking my coffee, I contemplated my ugly disposition and then made a startling discovery. A new predicament had just arrived! And just as I was about to throw myself down on the floor in defeat, or possibly a tantrum, my husband came whistling in the door with the menacing stamp. But now the need for the blasted stamp seemed trivial compared to my new crisis. This new problem was bad. Very bad.

I had suddenly realized that when I mocked my neighbor's kid on the phone, the entire phone conversation was recorded! You see, for some time, her answering machine had been malfunctioning and recorded every conversation. Including mine!

My neighbor kept meaning to get her machine fixed, but hadn't thus far. "Oh why didn't she get it fixed?" I stormed around my house in panic, literally freaking out. What was I going to do?

If you think I handled myself poorly under the pressures of a late bill, just read a few more lines.

With terror embedded in my entire core, a new frenzy was about to consume me. I quickly explained to my husband about my whole morning and what I had done when I phoned my neighbor to beg for a stamp. He laughed at me and shook his head, telling me that what I did wasn't so bad. Well that didn't help my situation at all. To me, it was monumental! Unforgivable! Catastrophic!

Then calmly, he said, "Just explain it to her and she'll understand."

Didn't this man just listen to my whole story? "I can't do that," I shrieked in horror.

Suddenly, a plan formed inside my head. Yes, I'm one of those people who can, on-the-spot, come up with a plan in the midst of chaos and disaster. (I'm not saying they're always good plans, but I *can* deliver.) An example of one of my good plans is when I was a teenager; my boyfriend accidentally burned my mother's brand new one-hour old couch with his cigarette! *ALERT...ALERT...DEF-CON ONE!* Immediately, I went into rescue mode. See? Smoking really is bad! Anyway, I ran to the kitchen, grabbed one of my mom's One-A-Day vitamins and moistened it...the color was an exact match to the couch. I rubbed it over the burn and TADA! No black scorch mark.

Oh, I suffered for years over that incident, just waiting for my parents' discovery.

The good news is, yes, there is a God! A very fine and loving God as my parents never noticed the vitamin repair until they were giving the couch away years later to my daughter, of all people. And that is when I confessed to my ingenious remedy to the burn. My apologies for digressing here.

Getting back to my terrible-awful-bad deed regarding my neighbor's boy…I had devised a split-second plan and hurried to my daughter's room where I keenly commandeered her Walkie Talkies.

Like a criminal, I sat at my window and staked out my beloved neighbor's home, waiting for her to leave for work. I quickly gave my husband the run-down of "The Plan" and revealed his major role in it.

After asking him to recite "The Plan" back to me seven times, I felt we were ready to launch "Operation Undo Stupid."

His covert mission entailed breaking in to my neighbor's house (I like to call it an extended invitation as we did have possession of her house key for emergencies…and this *was* an emergency.) His main goal was to erase the incriminating evidence from the blasted answering machine. This, he had to do under the radar of my other neighbor, "Eagle Beak," who never missed a thing going down in the hood.

Like a good soldier, my dear husband took his Walkie Talkie and was off to fulfill his ridiculous mission.

From *Command Central*, I held my breath and watched my faithful warrior execute perfect serpentine maneuvers through the jungle toward the crucial portal. I used my Walkie Talkie to give him periodic updates to the whereabouts of Eagle Beak and a heads-up if my neighbor were to unexpectedly return home.

Laden in guilt, more shame penetrated my soul as we successfully carried out my un-noble mission.

As far as technology goes…it only gets worse. A word of caution…beware of butt dialing.

Written by Aspen Michaels

Dandelion Wine Press is currently seeking true humor short stories for future compilations. If you are interested, please see our website for submission guidelines. **www.dandelionwine.co**

DANDELION
WINE
PRESS